Foreword:

I am very honored to introduce Pastor Shawn Baker's book on "Church Growth". Pastor Shawn has been a part of my life since the age of thirteen and I have been a spiritual mentor and Dad in his life to the present. My impartation to Pastor Shawn, that which he received well as an accountable piece in his journey, was to pray daily, read the Word daily, develop a lifestyle of fasting, pray in the Holy Ghost and serve somewhere and somehow weekly in the Kingdom. I also told him to develop a daily discipline to read with personal application daily the verses of Matthew 6:33; moreover, Luke 2:52 as a practical lifestyle for God's favor upon him in the Kingdom. Pastor Shawn Baker has God's favor upon him because of his obedience. There is no better person or author to speak to church growth with excellence and a working produced model. This is true because of his personal church growth, leadership and lifestyle of strong, mature, Biblical foundation in the Word put into practice and proven.

Pastor Jake Jacobs

Director Church Ministries

Princeton Pike Church of God

Hamilton, Ohio

Contents

You do not need this book!

Or any other book!

All you need is one book, THE WORD!

But since you made it this far, you might as

well finish it!

Chapter 1 Shepherds Who Feed with Knowledge and Understanding

I believe every church leader needs to invest the proper time in prayer and self-reflection asking the Divine hand, which placed you where you are as a leader, some crucial questions:

1. What does growth look like?

2. What does growth look like for the ministry You have entrusted to me?

3. How does this growth impact my community and the nations of the earth?

As the answers come, so will your plan of action, vision and mission. For God's thoughts will always trump the enemy's plans for your community. Ultimately, we are talking about working where the Father is working (see John 5:17).

When God finds a man or woman who makes this

their mission, to hear and implement His thoughts, then will be brought about the saying that is written in Jeremiah 3:15:

And I will give you pastors according to mine heart, which shall feed you with knowledge and understanding.

Could we honestly stand before the Lord one day and say we ministered according to His heart? Could we boldly declare to Him we fed His people with knowledge and understanding of His ways and His desire? Moreover, could we confidently confess the plans we implemented on how to reach our families and cities for Christ were rooted in a response to His answers to our questions? What if I proposed to you that the knowledge God would like to impart to you and the understanding He would like to bring to you may be counter intuitive to all that you have heard and understood in your ministerial training?

Before we dive into the growth strategies of Heaven for ministry, let us keep this ever on our mind and pulsating within our heart: if our growth does not include growth in love and an increase of the culture of Heaven, we have missed the purpose of life. The purpose of life is described in one word, LOVE (see 1 John 4:8). God does not just have love for humanity, He is LOVE!

To become Christ-like is to love like Christ. Furthermore, everywhere Christ went the culture of the Kingdom was manifest. Condemned people were set free and overcome with love. Hungry people were fed. The sick and afflicted of the enemy became a liberated and whole people. If we are not growing in love and experiencing an increase of Kingdom culture, our labor is in vain.

In this short book we will tackle the cultural aspect

of growth and touch on a few other topics as well. To validate this proven growth strategy, I will share my personal testimony for everything Kingdom!

Ministry

Over the past 20 years, my wife and I have worked in and pastored several churches. In each of these ministries we remained committed to the Word and the principles you are about to study. We experienced no less than 300% increases in attendance, finances and ministerial outreach. Churches ranging from 200 in weekly attendance, began booming to 1,000 spread across three campuses with multiple services. In one particular church, we began with 20 laity in weekly attendance and expanded to two campuses with 600 plus laity in weekly attendance. Through a steady and consistent pursuit of knowledge and a balanced blend of Bible teaching and exhortation with the Kingdom being central of all we do, the Lord has blessed us. This is why we have decided to release this book with Psalm 23 being our guide.

Business

In 2010 we bought into a struggling real estate firm that was in desperate need of a divine turn around. Many of the principles regarding culture, vision, mission and divine growth strategies written within this book were applied. For the past 6 years the firm has experienced unprecedented growth. Though this book is more geared towards ministry, the principles of the Kingdom can work anywhere! As a matter of fact, we applied the same principles and strategies towards our nonprofit ventures and experienced unprecedented growth as well. We will need to write a book for marketplace leaders and provide the revelatory information we have received for those in a separate document.

Please know however that no book or past experiences of others will ever replace each of us hearing from God for ourselves. To that end, please allow this book to serve as confirmation to what Holy Spirit is speaking into your heart.

Chapter 2

The Secret to Growth Found in Psalm 23

A word to my fellow laborers....

We have discovered that these principles applied, prove to be the healthiest, most successful way to grow a ministry:

1. Sow the seed and be sure the grass grows.

2. Keep the grass green and the sheep will come for it.

3. He will cause His sheep to lie down in green pastures.

Always remember, where there is grass, there will be sheep. Let us break down the 23rd Psalm, using it as guide to the fulfillment of Psalm 127:1: *Except the LORD build the house, they labour in vain that build it.*

As we approach Psalm 23, ponder these

questions:

Where do you think the shepherd should spend his time? How does the Lord build his house? And how can we avoid vain labor? Let us take a look.

Psalm 23

1 The Lord is my shepherd; I shall not want.

2 He maketh me to lie down in green pastures: he leadeth me beside the still waters.

3 He restoreth my soul: he leadeth me in the paths of righteousness for his name's sake.

4 Yea, though I walk through the valley of the shadow of death, I will fear no evil: for thou art with me; thy rod and thy staff they comfort me.

5 Thou preparest a table before me in the presence of mine enemies: thou anointest my head with oil; my cup runneth over.

6 Surely goodness and mercy shall follow me all the days of my life: and I will dwell in the house of the Lord for ever.

Verse 1. The Lord is my shepherd; I shall not want. (HE TAKES CARE OF ME)

The revelation of this verse liberates every ministry leader from fretting over finances. David, a king, is making this statement through his kingdom filter. Kingdoms are required to care for their citizens. Unlike modern societies in the West, corrupt kingdoms, or corrupt dictatorships, true kingdoms are required to take care of their people. Before going any further, read the following verses:

For the LORD is our judge, the LORD is our lawgiver, the LORD is our king; he will save us.
Isaiah 33:22

Giving thanks unto the Father, which hath made us meet to be partakers of the inheritance of the saints in light: Who hath delivered us from the power of darkness, and hath translated us into the kingdom of his dear Son...

Colossians 1:12-13

But seek ye first the kingdom of God, and his righteousness; and all these things shall be added unto you.

Matthew 6:33

Do you realize God rules over a Kingdom? And upon salvation you are translated *not* into a figurative kingdom, but a literal one! This is a literal kingdom with real benefits, which causes every man to press into it upon coming to an understanding of what those benefits are (see Luke 16:16). Psalm 103:1-5 captures just a few of the benefits of being a citizen within the Kingdom of God. An entire book could be dedicated to just the benefits of citizenship to Heaven.

Psalm 103 *1 Bless the Lord, O my soul: and all*

that is within me, bless his holy name.

*2 Bless the Lord, O my soul, and **forget not all***

***his benefits**:*

3 Who forgiveth all thine iniquities; who healeth all

thy diseases;

4 Who redeemeth thy life from destruction; who

crowneth thee with lovingkindness and tender

mercies;

5 Who satisfieth thy mouth with good things; so

that thy youth is renewed like the eagle's

(emphasis added).

As you can see, God offers a tremendous health

care plan! He is a benevolent King and this short

list of benefits exemplifies the purity and

awesomeness of a Holy Kingdom.

Isaiah 33:22 also reveals some insightful truths about the Kingdom. God is the embodiment of the Judicial, Executive and Legislative branches within the Kingdom. As a benevolent King and Ruler of the universe, He is well able to take care of His citizenry. However, most lack the revelation of the Kingdom because they have been taught to postpone it to some future event. No man has ever appropriated something he/she postpones. Jesus promised us in Luke 17:21 that the Kingdom of God is within us now and it is surrounding us (see the Amplified Version). The goal is to get the reality of what is abiding in our hearts to manifest in the seen world. The Kingdom of God is within you. God's Kingdom is designed to bring us into everything we need, independent of what is going on around us. This is called living life from the inside out! When this principle is understood, hearts will be overjoyed.

Paul gave thanks to the Father of our Lord Jesus Christ, who translated him into the Kingdom of His dear Son upon his surrender to Him while on the road to Damascus. As a fellow citizen, Paul could abase and abound while remaining content in either state. Why? Because the King is faithful to provide and meet the needs of His citizens. *I shall not want*! I always have enough each day to fulfill Heaven's desire in the earth. ***Our ministerial assignment is not tied to money, money is tied to our assignment!*** The King personally funds His desires; this is why it is crucial to consult Him about growth. He will bless His work!

Furthermore, as we seek first the Kingdom, the King provides revelatory knowledge and insight into His ways. As we gain understanding and begin to posses the wisdom on how to accurately articulate and impart the knowledge we are growing in, the King increases the value of His gift to the body (see Ephesians 4:11). Every ministry leader is a gift to the body. Some gifts are very valuable due to the treasure trove of insight they possess (see Matthew 13:52).

The greater the understanding of the Kingdom, there is less vain toil. The greater the understanding of the Kingdom, the greater the peace. Understanding and revelation of this key reality will ultimately determine where the ministry leader spends his/her time. They who lack it, their calendar will reflect it. Some leaders go from one meeting to the next, in order to keep their work going. I know this pressure and I completely understand! There was a season of ministry in my life that reflected this trap of the enemy. Activating these truths is so easy, we miss it. Take another quick glance at Matthew 6:33. As we seek the Kingdom, the Lord adds all things to us. All things simply means ALL THINGS!

If the revelation of Kingdom citizenship coupled with its benefits will take root within us as leaders, it will automatically trickle down to those who are following. And there is nothing more attractive than a community of people who live carefree, who are intentional about loving others and who manifest a peace that surpasses all understanding!

When this culture becomes the reality in which I personally live as a leader, others will begin to enter in with me. King David was clearly speaking of the King whom he served when he made the statement, *The LORD [Sovereign, Ruler, Owner, and King] is my shepherd, therefore I shall not lack.* **Only non-citizens of the Kingdom focus on lack.** As a matter of fact, this is what they fret about day in and day out (see Matthew 6:32).

Gentiles are non-citizens of the Kingdom, spoken of here.

I have truly experienced this reality. As I, a minister of the Gospel of Jesus Christ, walk in this reality, God has increased the men around me like sheep, like a mighty flock (see Ezekiel 36:37). Why? How? Verse 2 in Psalm 23 holds the key: *He maketh me to lie down in green pastures...* Always remember this principle, where there is green grass there will be sheep!

The Father causes His people to lie down in green pastures. Green represents the freshness of His word. John 6:63 states: *It is the spirit that quickeneth; the flesh profiteth nothing: the words that I speak unto you, they are spirit, and they are life.* The flesh profits nothing. The Word is what gives life and this truth confirms two points of affirmation. First, if the Word gives life and profits, we should invest our time here. Second, if the Word gives life, the God who is the Source of all life will lead His people where He is! Did you catch that? God is in His Word! Every Word of God that is received by faith is just as powerful as God Himself! This truth lies in the realm of the Spirit; there is no separation in the realm of the Spirit between God and His Word, they are one.

If the Word received by faith is just as powerful as God Himself, then let us re-read Matthew 6:33: *But seek ye first the kingdom of God, and his righteousness; and all these things shall be added unto you.* He said *all things.* This covers everything from finances to sermon material. This level of understanding cannot be denied! Herein lies the difference between those who seek a move God in their city or who become that move! Holy Spirit is an unstoppable force, the Word is Spirit and God is in His Word; therefore, every time we release the Word we are releasing an unstoppable force in the earth.

Revelatory insight of present truths (see 2 Peter 1:12) is what God desires His people to be established in. Furthermore, unveiling the revelatory insight of Heaven should be dispensed every time a man or woman steps into the pulpit! When this happens, God will begin to draw His sheep to this field, thus causing them to lie down in the field. Our responsibility is to the Word and prayer until the green grass begins to grow and until the fresh revelation comes. Keeping the grass green must be a priority! Where the grass turns brown the growth fades.

Earlier we discussed the importance of culture. Take note of part b in Verse 2: *...he leadeth me beside the still waters.*

The Good Shepherd is not only seeking to cause

His sheep to rest in the reality of His Word (green pastures), but He also is seeking to lead them beside the still waters. Still waters represent unity, peace and no division. This is where God desires to lead His sheep. Only you can determine in an honest manner if your culture is representative of still waters. Do people leave your service saying this church environment feels like heaven? They should. Do they leave your church saying that was the friendliest church in the world and the peace I felt was amazing? They should. Do they leave with their hearts burning within themselves (see Luke 24:32)? They should. Every person, from the saint to the demonized, should be able to rest in the abiding peace of His presence.

We read in Proverbs 25:11: *A word fitly spoken is like apples of gold in pictures of silver.* Do you see the contrast between gold and silver? There is a clear contrast in a ministry that is being dominated by the calming effect of the Word and presence of

God. Storms are calmed, peace prevails and the Word, which is fitly spoken, liberates hearts. Job said it like this in Job 6:25: *How forcible are right words*! God's Word is forcible and it is unmerciful to the powers of darkness; driving back the wind and the waves, until the environment on your Sea of Galilee becomes as a sea of glass just like it is before His throne in Heaven (see Revelation 4:6, Mark 4:39).

Chapter 3 The Impact of Green Grass and Still Waters

When the first three conditions of Psalm 23 are met, the outcome is glorious. The leadership is walking in the revelation of the Kingdom and making manifest its culture. The Word being dispensed is fresh. The environment is free of the toxicity of darkness. Then, people will leave your services proclaiming verse 3: *He restoreth my soul.*

This precisely describes the cultural impact of our faith community upon those who experience the Kingdom and encounter it. An atmosphere where souls can be refreshed, renewed and overcome with the culture of heaven.

A soul is restored by the washing and refreshing effect of the Word on the hearer. Paul describes this scenario using the relationship of a husband and wife yet speaking of Christ and His church (see Ephesians 5:26).

A soul that has been restored is the byproduct of a renewed mind.

Romans 12:1-2: *I beseech you therefore, brethren, by the mercies of God, that ye present your bodies a living sacrifice, holy, acceptable unto God, which is your reasonable service. And be not conformed to this world: but be ye transformed by the renewing of your mind, that ye may prove what is that good, and acceptable, and perfect, will of God.*

The word *transformed* in Romans 12 is the same word in the Greek, μεταμορφόω *metamorphoō*, used to describe what happened to Jesus in Matthew 17:2. **As the mind is transformed by the Word, the soul is transfigured!** We must understand, the Word of God was not designed to solely educate us but to conform us into the image of Christ. As this transformation takes place, the impact on the soul is glorious.

Our aim is to live with the mind of Christ. Any individual living outside the mind of Christ is a mind that is in languish. When we possess the mind of Christ as the Apostle did (see 1 Corinthians 2:16) we can live by the faith of Christ. There is a difference between living by faith *in* the Son of God and living by the faith *of* the Son of God. Many never cross this spiritual threshold. I believe beyond this threshold is the passageway into the supernatural realm. In Galatians 2:20 the apostle Paul makes this clear distinction when he said: *I am crucified with Christ: nevertheless I live; yet not I, but Christ liveth in me: and the life which I now live in the flesh I live by the faith **of** the Son of God, who loved me, and gave himself for me* (emphasis added).

What is even more interesting is found in the following verse, verse 21: *I do not frustrate the grace of God.* He is implying the divine enablement of God is hindered by the individual(s) who fail to cross this threshold due to a lack of revelation.

In conclusion, the mind is completely restored upon experiencing this transforming anointing which transfigures and restores the soul. It is here, in this state, that a person can live a life where their whole being exemplifies Heaven's purpose being made manifest in the earth realm. The soul is restored as the inner-man receives strength and nourishment. God, who is Spirit, leads His people through their spirit. When your inner-man/spirit is malnourished, your soul (the seat of your emotions, will and intellect) becomes overwhelmed. God's design was for our spirit to be led by His Spirit, versus our lives being dictated by our feelings. The soul ultimately finds its security under the leadership of Holy Spirit.

Let us further explore this truth in part b of verse 3: *...he leadeth me in the paths of righteousness for his name's sake.*

Now the hearer has come to the place where they see the Kingdom (see John 3:3).

Upon seeing the Kingdom, the believer, the lay leader, the congregational leadership and executive leadership truly see everything is about His name's sake.

Jesus' mind has not changed regarding this issue. Just as He made it all about the Father, we are to walk in the same Spirit. The precedent set by the Lord is clearly seen in Matthew 19:17: *And he said unto him, Why callest thou me good? there is none good but one, that is, God: but if thou wilt enter into life, keep the commandments.*

Furthermore, we see this in the Lord's prayer in Matthew 6:9-10: *After this manner therefore pray ye: Our Father which art in heaven, Hallowed be thy name. **Thy kingdom come. Thy will be done in earth,** as it is in heaven* (emphasis added).

The list of examples are endless. The point being, everything was and still is for *His* name's sake! This is the spirit in which we, as leaders, are called to lead by. Our teaching is Theo-centric pointing to the Blessed Potentate, the Senior Bishop and Overseer of our souls, Jesus the Christ! Everyone who leaves our assemblies should know we are communities where everything is about His name, His will, His desire, His purpose, His ministry, His plan, His Gospel and His heartbeat for the hearer.

What is interesting to me as a senior leader is

even when the first three verses of Psalm 23 are carried out to their fullest extent, we still have to contend with the bitter experience of verse 4.

What I love about the bitter experience is not so much the experience, but the outcome of the experience. All of us come to learn we have the greatest opportunity to experience God's goodness in the darkest hours of life. Sometimes our dark experiences are more about God's purpose than ours. The prison experience for Joseph was no doubt a dark one. The outcome? God's purpose being fulfilled for the earth! We can conclude Joseph's experience happened for His (the Father's) name's sake.

Our bitter experiences are always tied to the promise of Romans 8:28: *And we know that all things work together for good to them that love God, to them who are the called according to his purpose.*

Chapter 4 Being in the Center of God's Will and Walking Through the Valley of the Shadow of Death

Psalm 23:4 *Yea, though I walk through the valley of the shadow of death...*

Ministering in a place where God's presence is felt and experienced week in and week out in your services, does not exempt you from seasons of temptation. As a matter of fact, Hebrews 5:8 proves this was true even for Jesus: *Though he were a Son, yet learned he obedience by the things which he suffered.* We understand that a servant is not above his master, nor does our preaching lead people to believe we are exempt from hard times. We do however humble ourselves in the valley and recite 1 Peter 1:6: *Wherein ye greatly rejoice, though now for a season, if need be, ye are in heaviness through manifold temptations.* Manifold simply means many; many folds to the complexity of what you are confronted with. This is something we cannot explain in one or two sentences to our prayer partner. It is bigger than that, it is a valley! We have each been there.

I want to take a minute to remind you of an amazing Biblical truth. This truth has to do with your position in the Kingdom presently. First, let us understand what we are warring against and the hierarchy of the enemy's kingdom portrayed in Ephesians 6:12:

For we wrestle not against flesh and blood, but against principalities, against powers, against the rulers of the darkness of this world, against spiritual wickedness in high places.

Notice the breakdown of the hierarchy of Satan's kingdom. Satan sits at the top. The rank and responsibility of those underneath him are depicted here:

Satan - Chief

Principalities - Rule over nations or kingdoms (e.g. Daniel 10:13)

Powers - Rule, influence or control earthly governments and derive their authority from Principalities (e.g. Romans 13:1)

Rulers - Dictate culture and derive their authority from Powers (e.g. Luke 23:35)

Spiritual Wickedness or **Wicked Spirits** – Wicked Spirits desire to torment individuals and they derive their authority from Rulers (e.g. Mark 1:23)

Thus, we see the hierarchy of the Kingdom of Satan. But there is a powerful truth, seen in Ephesians 1:19-22, regarding our Lord Jesus Christ and the Father's work through the Spirit when our Lord was raised from the dead:

And what is the exceeding greatness of his power to us-ward who believe, according to the working of his mighty power, Which he wrought in Christ, when he raised him from the dead, and set him at his own right hand in the heavenly places, Far above all principality, and power, and might, and dominion, and every name that is named, not only in this world, but also in that which is to come: And hath put all things under his feet, and gave him to be the head over all things to the church.

This is not the revelation, but rather the foundation upon which the revelation must be received. Jesus, when raised from the pains of death, was raised FAR ABOVE Satan and his kingdom. He is now seated at the right hand of the Father (see Romans 8:34, Ephesians 1:20, Hebrews 1:3, 8:1, 10:12, 12:2).

Here is the revelation and the truth every believer must remember when he/she is walking through a valley. The revelation is found in Ephesians 2:5-6: *Even when we were dead in sins, hath quickened us together with Christ, (by grace ye are saved;)* **And hath raised us up together, and made us sit together in heavenly places in Christ Jesus** (emphasis added).

Do you see this? Can you see your spiritual position? You, right now, even in your valley are seated far above the entire hierarchy of the kingdom of darkness! You are seated in heavenly places in Christ Jesus. Praise the Lord!

It is in the valley when we rise up and proclaim, "I am not fighting *for* victory over this situation; I am fighting *from* a seat of victory!" It is in the valley when we rise up and proclaim, "I will fear no evil for my life is hid with God in Christ."

It is in full view of this revelation one fears no evil!

It is in full view of this revelation one can remain at perfect peace and be comforted by the reality of their state. In the power of this revelation we proclaim, "Thy rod and thy staff they comfort me."

If the enemy can blind God's leaders from this truth, he can stifle growth. However, the man who can see this will conform to the reality of what he/she beholds. It is very simple: what you see, you believe. What you believe, you supernaturally become. As the people we lead see this truth in us, it bolsters confidence in them. Elisha saw something in Elijah. Timothy saw something in Paul. And Peter saw something in Jesus; upon which Jesus proclaimed, *Blessed art thou Simon Barjona for flesh and blood hath not revealed it unto thee, but my Father which is in heaven* (see Matthew 16:17). What Peter saw, he believed. And what he believed, he supernaturally became. *And I say also unto thee, That thou art Peter...* (see Matthew 16:17). This is the becoming of what he saw! Simon became *Peter* (Greek, *Petros*, like the rock or Greek, *Petra*, i.e. Christ).

Chapter 5 Preparing Meals in an Unhindered Fashion

I have titled this fifth chapter "Preparing Meals in an Unhindered Fashion" for a reason. Every church leader is guilty of allowing circumstances of life to rob them from hearing the voice of God, thus preventing them from delivering fresh manna. Each of us know first hand how painful it is to minister or lead when you have not spent the time in the secret place like you should have. Or your time in the Word was not sufficient because of the demands of life and ministry. When the demands of life (i.e. your calendar) keeps you out of the secret place or from the Word, you are in a valley!

David declares in Psalm 23:5: *Thou preparest a table before me in the presence of mine enemies.* There are two points to glean from this passage. First, God still expects to meet with you and feed you in moments when you think the time is not right or you do not have the time. Second we, as under shepherds, should take the same approach afore mentioned and be sure our people have a spiritual table prepared for them.

Do our parishioners anticipate, each and every time they come in to the House of God, fresh manna in the face of their adverse circumstances? Can they expect the table to be prepared for them even when they are aware their pastor is fighting a battle? Remember, they see this in us first.

When we as leaders defy our personal struggles or life challenges by walking in the reality of our position, it makes it much easier to prepare a table for the hungry. Regarding the people, the better the food the greater the demand. In the last two churches I pastored, our people protected my time, rather than hijack it. I will admit, in times past I would feel a little disconnected or insecure if my people were not in constant contact with me. Today, when this is the reality, it serves as a great reminder that the Word is working and insecurity has no place in my mind! Unfortunately, most of our time as church leaders is spent managing what we think the people want versus what they need. Nothing will replace the anointing. Nothing will serve as a greater marketing program or community builder than the anointing. God anointed Solomon with wisdom. The Spirit of Wisdom went before him and caused the Queen of the South to come and see for herself. Jesus' fame was spread abroad, for never a man spake as he did, they concluded (see Matthew 12:42, Mark 1:28, John 7:46). In these two cases and many more in scripture, the anointing caused hungry, hurting people to press into what God was doing and saying. The same is still true today.

The anointing elevates the believer in every capacity. The anointing elevates the teacher and the student. I will share an intimate experience I had with the Lord early on in 2016. In John 14:21 Jesus said: *He that hath My commandments and keepeth them, he it is that loveth me; and he that loveth me shall be loved of my Father, and I will love him, and will manifest Myself to him.*

Keeping this verse in mind, I was driving one day when I immediately sensed the divine presence of the Lord in my vehicle. The question was posed to my heart, "Do you know what My anointing is?" I have learned throughout the years, when God asks a question, He is looking to give an answer and not necessarily receive one. My response was, "Tell me Lord!" He proceeded to enlighten my heart with these words: **"The anointing of the Holy Ghost is the sovereignty of my Spirit, breaking through your natural senses,**

enabling you to see, hear and operate in the supernatural realm".

When this answer was spoken into my heart, I did not need to pull over and get a pen and a piece of paper, in the case I would lose it; rather, it was forever etched upon my heart. When we as church leaders abide in the anointing our parishioners will say, "I can come to the House of God and eat fresh manna". They will leave proclaiming, *Thou anointest my head with oil; my cup runneth over.*

I love the statement, "my cup runneth over." It implies we are to minister from a state of overflow, not fullness. Likewise, our congregants are to receive to the point of overflow, not just fullness.

We can easily conclude that a head, which has been anointed by the sovereign Spirit of God, is a mind that has been renewed. Renewed minds effectively cultivate the culture of the Kingdom while representing Christ in an attractive manner. Most congregational leaders want to make Christ unavoidable in their communities. However, **the Kingdom approach is to make Christ irresistible!** Only a people with a renewed mind can truly make Jesus irresistible. When cultivating this reality, people begin to press into what God is doing in your assembly. The scripture states in Luke 16:16: ...*every man presseth into it.* Amongst every socioeconomic background, ethnic background, etc. the anointing attracts all and the renewed mind embraces all.

We stated earlier that sheep gather where the grass is green and they will scatter where the grass fades. Keep the grass green and the Good Shepherd will cause them to lie down, which leads us to our final point.

Chapter 6 - Divine Retention

Psalm 23:6 *Surely goodness and mercy shall follow me all the days of my life: and I will dwell in the house of the Lord for ever.* Part a of this verse implies that congregants are to be leaving church service with the right perspective! However, in this chapter I want to focus most of our attention on the latter part of verse 6: *...and I will dwell in the house of the Lord for ever.*

So much of our time and energy is spent on retention: providing people with opportunity, plugging them in and making it hard to relationally leave and find a new house of worship. Wouldn't it be something if our people were committed to the house of worship with a generational perspective? God thinks in terms of generations. He stated repeatedly, "I am the God of Abraham, Isaac, and Jacob" (see Exodus 3:6 as an example). The only way for the house of worship to become a generational house is for the sheep to encounter the Good Shepherd. Moreover, the following generation needs to witness our response to the revealed Word of God; to behold our hearts being captivated by the revealed truth and thus becoming prisoners of hope. Everything in ministry should be a byproduct of divine encounters centered on the Word.

I find it interesting that in most circles we desire for everything else to lead to divine encounters: our life groups, our mission trips, etc. When in all actuality the very thing that caused people to stick with Jesus were His Words. For example, in John 6:68: *Then Simon Peter answered him, Lord, to whom shall we go? thou hast the words of eternal life.* **Wherever the Spirit of Revelation is, there will be retention.**

If the Word cannot hold a person, we are all in trouble! The only pressure we should feel as leaders is the commitment and resolve burning within each of us to accurately release the heart of God in the moment. There is a passage in the epistle of James that I believe is key to retention. James 1:21: *Wherefore lay apart all filthiness and superfluity of naughtiness, and receive with meekness the engrafted word, which is able to save your souls.*

The word *engrafted* used here is a very dynamic word and one worthy of much consideration. *Emphytos* is the Greek word used and for one to understand the full strategic use of this word, we must think in medical terms. For example, when an individual is burned on one part of their body, the medical burn unit will remove healthy skin from a good part of the person's body and perform what is commonly referred to as a skin graft. The newly implanted skin must be nurtured and cared for over a period of time until it *takes*. With this in mind let us revisit James 1:21.

We could translate the verse in this manner: *Wherefore lay apart all filthiness and superfluity of naughtiness, and receive with meekness the engrafted* [implanted] *word, which is able to save your souls* [upon taking].

Our faith determines whether or not the Word *takes*! Once the word takes, the graft is set. Some people hear the Word but the graft does not take because the Word they heard was not mixed with faith. In Hebrews 4:2 we read: *For unto us was the gospel preached, as well as unto them: but the word preached did not profit them,* ***not being mixed with faith in them that heard it*** (emphasis added).

What happened in the example above? The graft

did not take and therefore the soul was not saved.

Can you imagine the outcome of an entire

assembly of believers who were walking in this

revelation? When they step into the sanctuary,

they do so, in faith believing and ready to receive.

What if every church leader stepped into their

leadership role operating in the same measure of

faith? They see themselves being used by Holy

Spirit as a doctor who is about to perform a skin

graft on a patient. The skin they use is the Word

of God! When faith is mixed with the hearing and

the delivering of the Word, the outcome is always

salvation! Anything that *takes* is guaranteed to

bring a Kingdom manifestation.

I am learning more each day what it is that

ensures the generations to come to continue in the

path we are paving. It is not based on what they

hear, but on what they see. Did they see the Word

work in our lives? Did they see the graft take? Is our faith real on this level? Like David, let us boldly declare Psalm 102:18: *This shall be written for the generation to come: and the people which shall be created shall praise the Lord.*

Everything Holy Spirit is writing (engrafting) upon our hearts is not just for us, but for those to follow! Therefore, we decree, "I (and my seed, to a thousand generations) will dwell in the house of the Lord forever!"

Chapter 7 Conclusion

Psalm 23

1 The Lord is my shepherd; I shall not want. [He takes care of me.]

2 He maketh me to lie down in green pastures: [He leads His sheep where there is fresh grass or fresh revelation of His Word] *he leadeth me beside the still waters.* [He leads His sheep where unity is common.]

3 He restoreth my soul: [It is in that place of unity and kingdom culture where souls are restored] he leadeth me in the paths of righteousness for his name's sake. [The kingdom life is all about the King's desires, wants, ways and will.]

4 Yea, though I walk through the valley of the shadow of death, [Being committed to the first verses of this Psalm in your ministry does not exempt you from dark valleys.] *I will fear no evil:* [The mind of Christ knows no fear and His mind gives peace to endure the dark valleys and the confidence to forge ahead! This describes us when we are walking in the revelation of our spiritual position.] *for thou art with me; thy rod and thy staff they comfort me.* [AMEN!]

5 Thou preparest a table before me in the presence of mine enemies: [External circumstances cannot keep us from receiving or dispensing revelation nor can it hinder the parishioner from receiving, if they are walking in the same Spirit of Revelation.] *thou anointest my head with oil; my cup runneth over.*

6 Surely goodness and mercy shall follow me all the days of my life: and I will dwell in the house of the Lord for ever. [God has a generational perspective. Parents, may you always remember that it is not necessarily what you will do that will make a difference in the Kingdom, but who you raise!]

I think it is important to remember whatever is growing in your congregation is exactly what is being planted. As leaders we carry the authority to bind or loose, to permit or to refuse good seeds or bad sees from being planted in our gardens. Your ministry is a garden! You cannot tolerate weeds nor allow weeds to be planted in your garden. People who know me well, know it is unacceptable to plant weeds in my garden by speaking things contrary to the Word of God. An individual will always speak what is in their heart.

This is why the Apostle Paul stated in Colossians 3:16: *Let the word of Christ dwell in you richly in all wisdom; teaching and admonishing one another in psalms and hymns and spiritual songs, singing with grace in your hearts to the Lord.*

Our assemblies should be rich with the Word. It is our job to passionately lead people to the Word;

inspiring them to become students of the Word by your pursuit to know the God of the Word. Inspire them to hide the Word in their hearts by allowing them to witness the Word freely flowing from you. The Word, according to 1 Thessalonians 2:13, is what effectively works in those who believe: *For this cause also thank we God without ceasing, because, when ye received the Word of God which ye heard of us, ye received it not as the word of men, but as it is in truth, the Word of God, which effectually worketh also in you that believe.*

Why so much emphasis on preaching the Word? First and foremost, it works! Second, we should understand the Kingdom of God will manifest where the Word of God rules! If the Word of God rules our hearts, then the Kingdom of God will manifest through our lives. Ultimately, that which is in hearts will determine the atmosphere. Again, let the Word of God dwell in your hearts richly!

The Word is referred to as seed multiple times in scripture. As a matter of fact, it is referred to as an incorruptible seed. This means it is not subject to decay (see 1 Peter 1:23, Matthew 13:18-23, Luke 8:11). When this seed called the Word of God is sown in our hearts by faith, it will keep us from sin (see Psalm 119:11).

The heart is likened unto a farmer's field. Whatever he sows in his field is the harvest he can anticipate. Jesus said, *A good man out of the good treasure of the heart bringeth forth good things* (see Matthew 12:35). Solomon said, out of the heart flows the issues of life (see Proverbs 4:23).

To this end we can conclude, our future will not be dictated by circumstances, our future is in our heart! By changing what is in your heart will actually change the shape of your future: shaping lives and making destinies sure by the seeds we sow. This is the bottom line: the Word works (1 Thessalonians 2:13); we just do not work the Word enough, nor do we allow the Word to work in us.

I believe this is how Jesus builds His church today, through people who pray the Word, preach the Word, sing the Word and ultimately live out the Word. He said in Matthew 16:18: ...*I will build my church.* The Lord is still in the habit of creating realities and building His church by His Word. May it be said of us from the generations to come, "We have never heard the Word celebrated so much in our lives!"

Made in the USA
Columbia, SC
05 September 2017